Parables

Poetry of the Mind

Ryan Ranney

PARABLES

© 2016 by Ryan Ranney. All rights reserved.

All words by Ryan Ranney
All Graphics and Images by Colleen Ranney
© 2004-2014 Ranney Studios - Ryan Ranney

Second Printing

PUBLISHED BY RANNEY STUDIOS

Books by
Ryan Ranney

Please send your comments or inquiries about this book by
visiting our website
or writing us an e-mail.

Website:

www.ryanranney.com

Face Book:

https://www.facebook.com/AuthorRyanRanney

E-Mail:

ryan@ryanranney.com

If you prefer, you can send a letter in care of the address below.
Thank you.

Ranney Studios
P.O. Box 125
Brussels Ontario Canada
N0G 1H0

Parables
Poetry of the Mind

Dedicated to God
to Wife and Family
to the Brotherhood and Sisterhood of Mankind

Table of Contents

Table of Contents

Foreword by Calvin Harasemchuk

"All men dream: but not equally. Those who dream by
night in the dusty recesses of their minds wake up in the
day to find it was vanity, but the dreamers of the day are
dangerous men, for they may act their dreams with open
eyes, to make it possible."
— T.E. Lawrence, *Seven Pillars of Wisdom: A Triumph*

*Parables is the awakening of the mind. Close your
preconceived beliefs, but not your mind, and you will
awaken. Take this journey of thought and understanding
from Ryan Ranney.*

*The best religion is the one that embraces the good in them
all, for those who do are indeed seeking understanding.
For it is in all of us to be good, we are taught to hate and
close our minds. An open mind is a loving one and has a
caring heart.*

*Parables is the first book of four from Ryan Ranney. To
truly understand all, you have to read all of his writings.*

*Ryan doesn't choose sides and has written with an open
mind and with deep compassion. For one to awake he
must first sleep and to dream one must have thought. For
one to speak he must have thought and have words. For
one to speak he must have an audience that listens, to
listen one must have an open mind.*

*Parables is that book which will open your mind and give
you a dream. You won't be disappointed.*

Calvin Harasemchuk, Poet and Author of "*Life, Love and
Heartache. Poems of the Northern Lights.*"
Calvin Harasemchuk can be found on Facebook.

Measure 1

To the Initiate

Don't Look Out the Window

You see it in the eyes of the wanderer
In the gaze of the soldier
In the stance of the homeless
In the cries of the insane
And in the mystical abyss
Of the true artist heart.

You see the desire for it
In the eyes of the protester
In the gaze of the lost
In the stance of the preacher
In the cries of the hurt
And in the abysmal hell
Of the drunkards heart.

But please don't look out the window
There is no going back
There is no return to former things
There is no wall to protect us
There is no way to forget
We cannot be saved
Once we look out the window.

You will stumble all the days of your life
Seeing no difference between the alley of filth
And the palaces of perfect splendor
Where prostitutes die by the ravages of men
And men die in the golden tombs of their wealth
Knowing there is no difference
Between the wall of standing frozen penguins
And the wall of walking men upon the street.

You will fester always in the knowing
That once we grasp a thing
It is no longer ours
And once we build a thing
It is for others

Don't Look Out the Window

And once we conceive a thing
It is a greater isolation on earth.

And what another has made
Will always be a greater retreat
Like a ride in the boat of a friend
Or an ancient Pyramid
Or a hidden Valley of the Kings discovered
Or the Grande Palace we once coveted with awe
Knowing now the master inside has no rest.

This is just information
This is just jargon and puzzles
To actually experience such an equilibrium
Of the absurd
Is to know that heaven is hell
And hell is heaven
In all that man does and hopes to do.

Yes it is true that none shall be free
No not one can be free
Unless they look out the window
But please don't look out that window
Until you are ready to let everything die
Like a pillar of salt upon the desert.

For no one shall ever appear the same again
And nothing shall ever be as it once was
And you shall never grasp what you once did
And you shall not be known as you once were
And you will know sorrow that cannot be known
In man's world.

Because there is no power in anything man does
Yet man believes
Even though the rebel and the conformist
Are the exact same man

Don't Look Out the Window

They believe they express power each
When there is no power in either.

The vanity of man's pursuit is overwhelming
And the fruitlessness is as a vacuum of space
And when they stand and say
SEE THIS GREAT THING I HAVE MADE
You will see the pattern of all men before them
Forgotten.

We are so entirely naked
Once we peer out the window
Without clothing, without armour
Without bones to stand
That none other than a God can be our companion
For now we get our first glance
At what God had made in secret
And what was unknown is known
While what was known is now unknown.

To be without our God outside the window
Would require immediate death
For none can stand in the surrounding truth
And live in lies.

None can breath the air of purity
And feed a rotten heart
None can taste the fruit of the spirit
And curse with their heart.

The fools think they are wise
And the wise know nothing.

To step outside is to cry out from the soul
While the tempest of the hardened heart
Softens to the pure silk of milk.

Don't Look Out the Window

And no one who fears to look out the window
Will ever believe ye sane again
Once you stare into the world that defined beauty
And harnessed eternity
And the place that actually has all Power
Even though it has no law but that of permanence
With Power enough to shackle the gate to hell.

The very gate with the window.

Do not look out the window
Unless you are ready to accept where you are
And where you have always been.

Ryan o0o

Measure 2

To the Vestige

Awakening Hidden Knowledge

Who can say what they saw
Or write what they heard
Or teach what they discovered
Or fix what is broken
Or break what cannot be fixed
In order to know it?

For it is that a mystery cannot be known
By using the tools of the known
And it cannot be that a secret is revealed
Given the knowledge already at hand

As he who trusts himself alone
Will find himself alone in his own ignorance
So to it is that she who beautifies herself alone
Will find herself alone in her ugliness

It is in order that for a tree to begin
Requires a tree
But from there must gain allies of strangers
The soil to protect it
The grit to activate it
The water to nourish it
The bugs to aerate it
The sunlight to empower it
The air and the earth and the sky
And all living things
To give it purpose

So too is this flow in the elements
So too is this flow in the animals
So too is this flow in humans
So too is this flow in the spirit
So too is this flow in the unknown

How many in life
Seek to know what they do not know

Awakening Hidden Knowledge

By using their own vision alone?

How many in life
Seek to know what has been given to another
By stealing from others what is theirs?

For in truth as a man, like the tree
I too require that which is strange to me
In order to know what I do not know
The unfamiliar

And in order to set out on my journey
Requires a tribe, a team, a band of explorers
Each and every one with their talents
Unknown to my ways

There I find my eternal family of life
In he who is a Priest
And he who is a Warrior
And she who is a Muse
And she who is an Oracle
And in they who are Crafters
And in they who are Laborers
And in they who are Growing
And in they who are Dying

It was let not that beyond this would be nothing
For also in the predator, the hunter, the prey
The greatest beast and the smallest creeping thing
Do I find counsel of mystery

And as it should not stop there
As it is also the love from my friends
The condemnation from my friends
Even love from my enemies
And the condemnation from my enemies
Where it becomes in light

Awakening Hidden Knowledge

For in these things are immense wisdoms
Of secret mysteries

As it is true in this life
That I will find myself in darkness
And find myself in light
So too are both of these our teachers

Even as I descend into madness
Or rise into the glory of perfected exactitude
Do I find clues along the way
All masterfully crafted to my own journey

Even pride is a gift
When we fall into humility
And when we rise into wisdom
Do we credit our foolishness

For I cannot gain in darkness
Surrounded by any such thing as myself
It was I who found myself there
And all like me would likewise be so

And I cannot gain in light
Surrounded by any such thing as myself only
It was I who got there by revelations of mysteries
And mysteries are revealed by another source

As the friend who is a Priest does consider
And the friend who is a Warrior does protect
And the woman who is a Muse does inspire
And the woman who opens Herself does heal
And the Crafter does provide
And the laborer does clear the path
And the growing do seek
And the dying do remember
So too do I have my part

Awakening Hidden Knowledge

Unlike them all

They are strangers to my ways
And friends to my heart
A family unknown to all others
That in time I shall be as the Tree

And as my feet have reached down deep
Into the ground
So too have my branches reached ever outward
To explore and touch and feel and know
Every flow of passing life
Every particle of drifting life
Every pleasure of intimate life
Every wonder of spiritual life
And every mystery of the secret life forgotten

This is the path

Since the Beginning

Peace cannot be bought with lies
Nor happiness with denial.

No man or woman can stand in the face of truth
and say they are Light.

They who smile at others in order to show their light
have exposed their darkness.
They who smile at others to hide their darkness have
revealed their dream of Light.

Who can escape their nature but for a little while
worship instead their image?

Is it not He who knows his truth
that carries a heavy stone?

Yet he and she are not the same!

We can look and study and search and wonder but
none of us will discover the one who knows their
truth. There is a soul protected by wisdom to play a
fool to be a god. As that one stares into our eyes they
are as any other man staring into the face of a beast.
He knows to be ruthless yet gentle, stern yet
understanding, open yet unwavering and kind yet
discerning.

If one can see a woman who appears to know her truth
then she is protected by them to be hidden away as a
precious jewel. Such it is with all riches that he who
flaunts his wealth shall lose it. He who exposes his
treasure will find his vaults plundered. That same man
tho who nurtures his soil and protects his borders will
even more grow many crops to share amongst the
whole world.

Since the Beginning

Such a man would have to first know himself and his truth, his joy and his destruction, his peace and his war, his pleasure and his sorrow. Such a man would have to know the horrors of his heart and all the heavenly things also placed there.

It is by the contentment in all that we have done do we mark the foundations of our soul.

It is not by the desires of eyes, or the happiness of what we posses. There is no end to the acquiring of things and no end to the desire to acquire. Therefore make record of all that you have done and inquire within yourself to what is good and what is not. Separate that which brought you joy from that which brought you regret. Do what honored you.

Be fearless in the pursuit of your truth for it will even still take all the remainder of your life to construct it. Why play the game of images? Why wallow in the mud of self-deceit and public approval? Not one other will lay their head on your pillow. Not one other will lay their body in your deathbed. Not one other can love the real you if you are not who you wish to believe you are.

When at peace, proclaim it
When humbled, accept it.
When wrong make it right.
When hurt let it be known to yourself.
If you find bliss, embrace it.
When you find awe, respect it.

All that you hide from yourself you expose to the world as a greater sickness except from those who are also ill.

Since the Beginning

We are of both light and dark, life and death, peace
and war.

But the liar who lies to himself is as the one without
any portion of himself.

The flesh does wither as the soul does grow
And when the soul and flesh wither together
Then who can arrest the grave for us?
Even before our time are we as dead.
This too must we admit if it is so.

Only they who come out of darkness can live in light.
Only they who know their darkness can leave it.

Who can dig a whole without making a pile of dirt?
Indeed who can fill a hole
without removing a pile of dirt?

Measure 3

To the Accession

The Phoenix

How long does one walk
Down the darkened path
Of world discovery
Of self discovery
Of the discovery of mankind?

We set ourselves above the land
Though the land does not lie
We set ourselves above the water
Though the water does not lie
We set ourselves above the animal
Though the animal does not lie

We set our minds above the stars
Though the stars do not know us

We set our hearts above the hearts of humans
Though every human has the same needs we do

We cause others to recompense our lives
Even though their debt is larger than ours

We accuse others of our unhappiness
Yet praise ourselves of our happiness

We hide who we are
Even from ourselves
In a universe that knows the truth
In a universe that lives only by truth

Sing a song
Upon the stage of the world
Hide behind the veil
Drift along the river of doubt
Live beyond the shore
Of delight

The Phoenix

Love the reflection
Of your own creation
Stare into the abyss
Perfect the image of falsehood
Until a ripple of truth
Upsets the mirror

None can see the enemy
While staring right at him

For every truth on earth
Is hidden behind two untruths
Even a third
Of our own making

And every discovery on earth
Is the cost of two
Even a third
Of our own coin

And every step in the spirit world
Where we must abide to endure
Awakens they who live in light
And they who live in darkness
Whereas our own awareness is the prize
Of a war we cannot fathom

Yet all around us it is
In the world
But this is also just a reflection
Of a lie

What choice do we have
But to live in the truth
And die in the truth
Or live in the lie
And die in the lie?

The Phoenix

So I will speak of the power forgot

I stand and say that I have power
As do all humans – as we live
Yet we are not the source of our own power
We are the carriers of that power

I look and see the power of the bear
As can be seen in all animals
Yet they are not the source of their own power
They are only vessels of power

I witness the power of nature and its results
As can be seen in all parts of the earth
Yet nature is not the source of its own power
It is only the action of power given to it

I did not create or evolve myself
Of my own power
Nor did the bear
Nor does the tide

Even the earth itself
Did not manufacture itself from nothing
Nor then give itself power from nothing to do so
This was by the force of something else

Even the Big Bang did Boom because of the power
given to it to do so

So then if I stand in praise of myself
I do lie in the speaking of my power
As my own source

And if I stand in accusation of another
I do lie in the speaking of their power
As their own source

The Phoenix

We are not the source of life
As life existed long before us
But we may live in it

We are not the source of death
As death existed long before us
But we may die in it

Life can be given by the Power of Life
And Death can come to that which is then living
But death cannot give power to death
For death is the end

Life is the beginning and the source
Of both life and death

All that is, has been, will be, and is dreamed of
Has a source from which it draws power

That source is life
Some call it God

The war is a reflection of a lie
Because even darkness draws its power from light
Until such time as the light puts all darkness away
Until such time as the light cuts off the power
To the dark

The lie is a robber and a thief
And it is not even the source of itself

The truth is the light and the pattern
Of the whole universe
And it is the source of all power

The lie keeps us in darkness – blind to all things
And it hates the truth

The Phoenix

The truth keeps us in sight of all things
Even the lie

The lie wants to be the truth
It wants to convince you
That it is the source of all power

A lie is designed to deceive you
Into believing
It is something that it is not
So that it can steal the power given to you by life

The truth is the source of all power
And it needs to convince no one

A truth is designed to relieve you
Of all lies
And darkness
And ultimate powerlessness

The phoenix did die unto its lies
And rose again from the ash of darkness
To soar in the light of the sky
Once more

One cannot die
Until they first live
And one cannot live
Without the TRUE source of all Life
The True source of all power

What then do you worship
The reflection of lies and its accuser
Or the reality of truth
That all other things live in?

A Star Dwellers Return

(Interpreted Symbology – Finding Earth Again)

Beautiful blue waters glow
The work of life revealed
Land below standing still
In this forgotten corner
Of the cosmos

Within her shores tempered rest
Call to my bones
Origins return of opening voices
Spoken unlike ever before
This realm forgets not

To things "as it is"

How can this be
Of low made upright
Walking man
While away there be few
Remembering her gardens?

It shall be as known is known
Throughout the heavens stare
Brought again into the hearts
That all bow
When awe takes the word

To things of "as it were"

There when distant travels prevailed
All kind of its kind
Poured out upon the earth
As trumpets pierce silence quiet
None could be found to command her

Just as delight found rest

A Star Dwellers Return

When the lion roared
So too is it also to be
Opened waters of man
With heart unable unknown

To things "as it will be"

Oh to see with eyes of life
Even more so with everlasting life
Not one little thing
Finds uncherished love
In the wisdom of it all

This that man shall know
His quiet embrace accepted
That which was him
Before his eyes
It is his will alive

To things "as is always"

Hear the temple alight its fire
To this one equation
Always never not always
Lit at the end
Burned always until the beginning

It is the way of love
That no aggressor can defeat
What exists only because of it
As two reflect
So does life reflect in only

That Which Survives

What does one have when everything's impermanent?
What does one know when everything is wrong?
What does one see when everything is blurred?
What does one hear when everything is silenced?

What are we really?
Are we just a self centered set of self justifying rules
designed to protect us from whatever it is we think we
really are?

Why must anyone be like me?
Even those who stand out the most
Do so in the light of adoration.
Even those who claim uniqueness
Do so in front of millions.

Why is it they strive so hard
To show us how different they are?

If no one needs to be like me,
Then no one needs to know they aren't.

If I am unique, your approval of that is not important.

What is this faith we seek?
Even those who enter churches
Do so to find what they have not
While those who do not enter
Seek to proclaim what they do not need.

Even those who proclaim the greatest faith in a god
Do so in fear of yours
while those who proclaim nothing
Do so in fear of god.

If one is truly in faith
There is no fear of another faith.

That Which Survives

When one is truly full
There is no fear of another's meal.

Why must we want for one another? (non romantic)
They who desire another to be as they wish
Are they not enough themselves?
They who want the love of another
Do they not have enough love themselves?
Why do we wish to know the love of those who do not
wish to give it, while we desire not the love of those
who do?

What is love anyway?
Even those who stalk another
With unwanted advances, believe they love us.
Even those who desire us, believe it is love
Just because of their want.
Even those who suffer that delusion
Believes we do also want them.
And who said it is love only if I give you
What you have determined I should?
If I must be as another wishes, for them to feel loved
Then it is not my love they seek, it is their own.

They who love me will seek to love my life
As i see fit to live it.
This respect we give to pets
Yet people we oppress to obey our vision of love!

Even he who claims to know love
Does so to share HIS vision of it!
How can that be your love?

I know of no other
Who has walked all the steps of my life
as I have never walked the steps of another
yet STILL do I believe in my opinions of you?

That Which Survives

And how truly can I hold fast to my beliefs?
Are they not one perspective among BILLIONS?
Are they not limited to shortened years?
Are they not proven wrong daily?
Only to have that proof wronged?
Are they not tested continually?

What of my experiences?
They are not with me... they are the past.
What of my hopes?
They are not with me... they are the future.
What of now?

In now is only my love for another.
Be a brother or sister
They are not here to know this love.
Be a father or mother
They are not here to know this love.
Be a son or daughter
They sleep knowing nothing of my love.
Be my wife, she too sleeps unaware of such passions I
have for her, until she rises to see them in my eye.

What do we have if we cannot give it?
What do we know if we cannot share it?
What do we see if we cannot envision it?
What do we hear if we cannot understand it?

I am deep in my love for another
And I am unafraid of who I really am
Because I love loving her
And I love her no matter who she is
As I love myself no matter who anyone thinks I am.

And I am deep in this love
Just because it is mine
To behold for her.

That Which Survives

I have never needed anyone or anything
Or any thought or any ideal
Or any image or any want
To love her.

It is only that love in me
That is permanent
That has never been wrong
That has never been blurred
That has never been silenced in my heart.

All souls grow old
All eyes grow dim
All purpose grows to other concerns.
All hearts for us can wane
Into the oblivion of the human epidemic.

What does not wane or falter or wash away or forget
or turn off, is the Love God put in our hearts for any
other who had shared their true love also with us.

It never dies,
Even in the realm of hell it thrives,
Even in the gates of Heaven it is as a Phoenix
Born over and over.
With every touch, every whimper
And every breath, it is.

This is the beauty of the heart
The heavy balance
And that which survives.

Measure 4

To the Founded

Only Human

If there are more things unseen than seen
and more things unknown than known
and more things unheard than heard
and more things unwitnessed than witnessed
and more things unthought than thought
and more things uncreated than created...

And if it is true
That there is nothing new under the sun

Wouldn't one be forced to reason

That all we know is actually false?
and all our logic is actually laughable?
and all we believe is actually speculation?
and all we feel is actually entertainment?
and all we judge is actually ludicrous?

And all our faith is actually based on nothing more

Than what we have been told to trust?
And feelings we like over feelings we don't?
And thoughts that we agree to because we like them?
And rules we obey because we fear punishment?
And masters who only Told us they were?
And this by people before us
who didn't even create these ideas?

Because this would mean our creations today
MUST have been created before
and lost before
as we lose them today.

And this would mean
something limited us
COMPLETELY
from ever expanding beyond

Only Human

the 7 stories we can tell
and the 7 thoughts we can hold simultaneously
and the 7 levels to our growths
and the 7 levels of our demises
and the 7 chakras of our bodies
and the 7 senses we can fathom
and the 7 notes we can hear

Because nothing new can be under the sun, even
though there is nothing here compared to what there
can truly be elsewhere in the unknown.

Imagine in trust
that ALL we do have
has been here before
and ALL we will create
was created also before.

What ideas have You had
and seen another prosper creating them?

What songs have you heard in your head
and then heard another wrote them?

What words have you thought
and then read another has written them?

Every generation before us
Dismissed or killed the men who spoke the truth
About washing hands in hospitals
About the center of our galaxy
About the roundness of the earth
About the nature of love
About the importance of nutrition
About the benefit of herbs
About the desire of freedom
About the LOVE of God.

Only Human

Yet we learn and confess and obey the generations
before us?

I submit to you
That if truly nothing is new under the sun
Then we are not progressing in time
Or in any other fashion.

We are indeed digressing
and turning back
and withering away
and repelling change
and fleeing anything
or any chance
of anything different
in any way.

Lather, rinse, repeat

All that we do, we do again

All that we have not done
we are already wanting to do
because somehow we already
know we will like it.

Even that which we do not want to do
we already know we don't want to do it
before having done it.

Perhaps we have done it before?
Perhaps it is nothing new?

And where can someone show me anything
other then our only two choices
of Life or Death
Blessings or cursing

Only Human

growth or decay
breathing in or breathing out
giving or taking?

Yet there are more WAYS to existence than these.
Just not under THIS sun, as a human.
There are more ways unknown, than known.

So with our Two choices,
and our 7 sources of input or output
Tell me who can teach?
and who can learn?
and who can create?
and who can destroy?
and who can speak and it is so?
and who can refrain of speaking and it is not so?

Surely not us
we lather rinse and repeat

We have fear or we have courage
of things that are not happening
in a place that knows very little
centered between our ears.

And we THINK we know what makes life, life
and what makes death, death.
And we THINK we know who is right
and who is wrong.
And we THINK we know
who is worthy and who is not.
Because we only have two choices under the sun.

Even HE who says ALL are worthy
speaks of one choice over the other.
Even he who says No one is worthy
speaks only of one choice over the other.

Only Human

Yet under another sun
are many more choices
available to anything
other than humans.

So who is to say
what is good for another
or bad for another?

We cannot even remember ALL the days
to our own lives
Yet we feel we have authority to judge
another life?

Perhaps we are just following the blind
blindly down the former things
reversed in time
that we agreed to
in order to be rewarded
by those who imposed the punishment
that was exacted on them?

Even our greatest men
have had great men before them
and will have great men after them
all doing the same things
over and over.

Even our worst enemy
had enemies before him
and will have enemies after him
all doing the same things
over and over.

I want for nothing new
because nothing new can be had
that hasn't already lived in my own mind

Only Human

or the mind of another
before or after me.

And this we also think we know

That the mind knows no difference
between what it sees in imagination
or what it sees outside itself.

So what is real?
and what isn't real?
When reality itself
cannot be fathomed at all
in the realm of humanity
given only two choices...

amidst the sea of the unlimited Universe of God?

And who can say anything of God,
that hasn't already been said
a million times over a million times?

Who can say anything about themselves
that hasn't already been said
a million times over a million times
by others?

Time has no Say in Losses

How can the hunger of a soul reflect anything less than the moment recalled or dreamed?

Is it not where we live?

Whatever we gain or whatever we loose is of itself a matter of a moment. One cannot hold power or strength or riches or glory or pride but for that moment. One cannot loose power or strength or riches or glory or pride but for that moment.

Persistence of anything physical is an illusion created by a magician who only needs a moment to convince you of an inevitability. Persistence of a law of man, a right of man, a principle of man or a condition of man is likewise nothing more.

Where do we not find the circular game?

Our histories show the rise and fall of every building, every race, every culture, every establishment, every ideal, every religion and every thing of man that man can know.

Our present confirms this.
Our future is the same.

Some shun their past; finding no value there. Others curse the dream of the future; trusting instead in their strategic perspective.

Yet do we not find our past lives on forever with just a simple recall?

And do not our dreams grow also with another simple imagining?

Time has no Say in Losses

It is here in the seat of the soul, in the chambers of the heart, in the corners of the working mind that eternity of every moment is given breath. It is then here in the realm of the waking world that touchable experiences lay down the path of our past and inspire our future.

Kiss someone you love and in an instant you will know this is true. See how after the moment it is there, in your soul, as a living past moment of wonder?
See how it sets your will to wish for more in the future?

Those who shun their past, fear their past or find nothing of value there, live only now in their flesh. Their soul does not gain strength or honor or wisdom. They dwell in a withering lie, for even their current belief was formed by the very past they lived. Without their past they would have no conception of non-value to judge their past.

If they look to the future they also form that dream according to the events of their past. They cannot hide from the past otherwise they cannot run to the future.

Those who shun or fear or find no value in a dream for a future also live as flesh in the moment only.

Yet who can say this in truth?

Ask any one who punishes a dreamer and they will tell you that they punish the lazy dreamer because their future will be in jeopardy without their guiding discipline! Hypocrites!

Even he who says he has no plans will then begin to tell you his plans of non-plans. Hypocrites.

Time has no Say in Losses

It is their soul that suffers the delusion that they cannot dwell upon tomorrow. It is this very lie that tries to hide the future in order to control the future that cannot be controlled without dreaming about it!

The lie to their soul corrupts all growth, suspends all maturity.

Who can be so lost? Yet everyday you will hear your fellows speak of these things.

Even men of power and prominence will stand before many saying such things.

Just look to the heavens with eyes of the scientist. You will see that even the stars came from somewhere and are there now and also going somewhere.

Everything moves, everything expands, everything breathes in and out.

Our past is the ingredients by which our present was formed. Our future is the product we create with those ingredients.

Without our past and without our dream
We Create Nothing.

They who live on the path of the soul
Must walk after the example of all living things.

We must live as eternal beings cherishing every moment before and every moment after.

We must also stand in the present as the creative-less do, but we must be creators as our universe is.

Time has no Say in Losses

THIS is what lives on. What else can live on unless what was before is known and what will be is sought out? Everything of man that man grasps is impermanent.

What is permanent is the soul that reaches out and touches all things before and after in their living experience. It is the heart that is weighed by the universe as living or dead. It is in the heart of man that the choice is planted.

One must dream of peace to create peace. One must have experienced war in the past to wish to dream of peace.

One must dream of intimacy to create intimacy. One must have experienced and honored their isolation of the past to embrace and discover intimacy.

One must dream of anything better
To create anything better.

One must respect and uncover and remember the sorrow of their past in order to assemble something better.

Time has no say in losses and truly no say in gains. Right with us right now is the power of all our steps before, and every step we choose from now on.

The End the War

Ask yourself why?
What purpose there is to know a lie?

I will say what I know

War has been staged - FOR US
Complete with weapons of
Envy
Hate
Fear
Jealousy
Racism
Sexism

Ask yourself again!

Who is it that supports your battle
but steals your victory?

Gain a foothold
Loose a loved one.

Gain an advantage
Suffer subversion.

Gain a Hope
Watch your resources fade.

Run and Hide... right into the enemies camp!

Stand and Fight... As your army flees behind you.
Leaving you alone to face your enemy.

Do you see this in your life?
Do you hear this in your prayers?
as you ask why!
Do you know this in your experience?

The End the War

Wish to defend your rights
and see how you lose them.

Wish to defend your Family
and see how they love your enemy.

Wish to seek justice
and see how it dawns a new war!

Is there no end to the intelligence
of the one who supports our Battle
Yet STEALS our Victory?

See..? Even we heal from our wounds
To Fight again!

When even we know by truth
that our aggressors are no match for us,
how is it they prosper at our expense
as we prosper at theirs?

If truly our human foes were the puppet-masters of
our demise, then why are we all given the same
weapons?
Wouldn't they keep the weapons all to themselves?

Yet a human who hates is hated by the hated
and the human who hits is hit by the one who's struck
and the human who yells receives strong words also
and the one who steals has nothing of their own
and the one who rapes has no love of their own
and the one who conquers has no one who has given
themselves to them.

All this that we would fight forever
NEVER finding eternal victory.
Even the ones we kill have sons who avenge.

The End the War

Who is it that supports your battle
but steals your victory?

What god knows how to command your every step
and stage your war all the days of your life?
That you should know strife always
and never find serene rest?

Will you fight to support this god who toys with you?

One Must Not Fight
Not Ever
Not Anything

Because every weapon placed in your hand
is done so by the enemy spirit itself.

How great a defeat we have
that the bomb of envy blows up on our soil
and the dagger of anger cuts our own hearts
and the strategy of prejudice
separates us from our brothers
and the army of fear attacks our own fortresses.

It is by design that you should fight
and fight also with the weapons your enemy crafted
for you!

So that it shall never be HE who is fought
but that we fight ourselves
with our own weapons we weld.

One Must Not Fight
Not Ever
Not Anything

The End the War

There once was a story of the God of gods
and the King of kings
Who Commanded that we have no other gods before
Him.

And he came to us
in this place of perpetual war and hell
and said...
"Do Not Fight, and you shall Win the War"
"Lay down your life, and you shall have eternal Life"
"Love your neighbor as yourself"
"Give freely and with a glad heart"
"In service we find brothers, and with brothers we can
recover from anything"

And he gave to us not weapons, but tools
of Love
of Generosity
of Freedom from judgment
of Truth
of Peace
of Laughter
of Miracles.

All around we see the beauty of Eden in all that the
Greatest God Made.

All around we see the plight of man suffering in Eden
at the hands of a lessor god.

For me to fight is to worship a lessor god
and he only promises war and destitution.

For me to embrace the beauty of Life
is to follow the God of gods
and He Promises me Eternal Life in Peace.

The End the War

I love that story
because it makes sense of all I have seen and know.

One Must Not Fight
Not ever
Not Anything.

Only a Fool Fights in a Burning House

I, like my Father before me
desire instead to Create
with these New Tools of Love.

Do No Harm

We cannot put away the beast
Unless the beast is first set free

Those who war and those who rage
Are those afraid to see what lies
Beneath the glare in their eyes

Rules give way to chains
And law gives way to obedience
And structure gives way to calm
While the planet dreams utopia
Without knowing ones self

How many times have you wanted to run?
Fast away from that life of yours
Fast away from the orchards of humanity
Fast away from the image of yourself
That others assigned we should be?

What a great thing it is to remain in the dome
Because most cannot fathom their beast
And indeed they themselves know
It is beyond their own control
It is the very release of any control at all.

That is what it is.

So where do we stand?
Are we kind in order to deny our shadow?
Are we lawful in order to avoid our will?
Are we nice in order to keep the taking of arms at bay?
When have you smiled with truth?

Look to the world
It is not satisfied with hiding any longer.
It will no longer obey it's master.

Do No Harm

The people are rising up
Against themselves
In order to overthrow their oppressor.

They are trying to set free the beast
Without any experience
They let lose the dog.
Now we see Nations at war with themselves
And Nations at war with Nations

I was one who ran to the woods
And let loose the beast
With fury and fire and rampage
It burned away every portion
Of every portion of my life.

The beast is as dark and deep and horrible
As is the light bright and high and beautiful.

I myself understood the need
For my own death

Even though I used to be a little boy
And full of love and grace
And the desire to laugh with you
Inside grew a relentless beast
And that beast is the same for us all
This is the meaning of mobs

None are free
Until they put away the beast they set free
Which is how we marvel not at war
And why we stand not in the way of sin
In order to have choice over the hell of our shadow

And this is where the image changes.

Do No Harm

The journey to peace is lead
By those who Mastered war
And did away with it.

None shall find peace following man's righteousness.

The path to liberation is laid by those who were slaves
And set down each rock of hell into the ground.
So that others may walk on solid ground and not sink.

None shall find liberation
By the government of the privileged.

Those who are just in the law
Are those who lived every form of lawlessness
In order to be the law they now do so love.

None shall obey law without honest respect.

Only a drunk of great magnitude
Can become sober minded to great magnitude

Only those who were tortured with fear
Can show the way to fearlessness.

Only the darkest heart, broken in the darkest hour
Will define the nature of Love to all the world.

This is why I have chosen Love
And why I have chosen Sobriety
And why I have chosen the Eternal Law
And why I have chosen Liberation
And why I have chosen Peace.

Because only the Dead shall Rise.

Do No Harm

My love is no vainglory
Nor is my peace mistaken
Even my liberation is unquestionable
And the law of my love for my Creator
Has no fathomable end.

Indeed the universe is beautiful beyond measure
And the brothers and sisters before me
Are deserving of life
Each and every one given their own name
And fashioned to their own face
Living a life that none other shall ever live
Unique and personal to every living soul

And though some will never lead
And some will never create
And some will never rise on earth
They were not meant to.

They were meant to know the light
Of not knowing darkness
In order to prove the power of light.

My desire is that you live
My desire is that you are given love
My desire is that you are given peace
My desire is that you are given liberation
My desire is that you fearlessly experience
Everything that may bring joy to your heart.

My desire is that no one should harm another.

Put away the beast
So that all may see your Rise to Life.

Measure 5

To the Efficacious

The Tasks of Man

What is this that man should be?
Our days are filled with tasks.
Our nights are filled with tasks.
Even our rest is overrun with tasks.

Who among ALL the men of earth has escaped?
I tell you not one alive has walked without his
multitude of errands and items. Not one rich, not one
poor, not one blessed, not one cursed, not one with
talent, or one without shall flee from this reality. Yet
perhaps only the mind that has been left a in
vegetative perception may be pardoned.

The order of man to protect himself, to feed himself, to
shelter himself has at the very least been within us.
Nature demands survival, and physical survival
demands our precious time. The hunting, the
gathering, the building, the searching, the labor of man
never ends. To be a man is to be a slave to our bodies.
Without rest it yearns for more, without end its needs
are made apparent. A new day brings a new
requirement.

As if this is not enough. In our epiphany we conceive
security to be found in the acquiring of our needs. Lest
we die of the elements, or starve in the garden we go
on. Then he who has amassed the most has now
perceived the most security. He who is lazy works
doubly hard to envy the one who has more. He who is
rebellious devises cunning to rob from another. All
now seek not the item of the task, but the security
given from the possession.

As if this is not enough. In our haste to gain we
establish rules to our conduct for he who has the most,
and he who has the least. In another great awakening
we commend civility to our nature and manners to our

The Tasks of Man

gestures. In comical vanity we display these ideas to ourselves knowing ALL the while they are that which has destroyed civility and conquered the giving spirit. Lies pour out of our mouths from fear of our place in this newly created man made set of tasks.

Mountain upon mountain of burdensome tasks we have created from one generation to the next. Conceptions, ideas, morality, rules, laws, ethics, peace and war all come from our damning destiny of task driven existence. Behold we teach our own minds to train our minds on these things. There is no end to the sky, and it shall never end. Man shall never be satisfied with that which he has to do.

The poor in wealth must slave to he above him. The poor in mind must burden his body to the undesirable work. The poor in body must educate himself to all the vanity of man's logic and reasoning. The poor in talent must humble himself to his fate.

The great in wealth is burdened by the meager. The formidable mind must discover the unknown. The strong in body must fend off the weak. The powerful in talent must endure all manner of evil.

He who commands must follow the conduct of another's ideal. He who serves must follow the conduct of another's ideal. Both must dwell also in the various tasks of their creation.

The man who looks to all his work and finds comfort there will grow old and not be able to accomplish it. The man who looks to all his things and finds comfort there will never cease to slave for more. The man who finds passion in drink shall lose all, and be bound to a greater task by those in authority. The rebel shall be

The Tasks of Man

tasked to rebel, the conformist shall be tasked to conform, the business man shall be tasked to do business, the artists shall be tasked to create, the laborer shall be tasked to labor. The powerful shall be tasked to maintain power, and the weak shall be tasked to maintain weakness.

In the end all men shall walk their lands, survey their homes, count their possessions, ponder their children, wither away and die. Nothing they have worked to do shall go with them where they go, and nothing they have done that they hold dear shall be remembered as they beheld it. The mighty will look upon their empires with the feeling it wasn't enough, and the small shall look upon their lives as well with the same conclusion. The yin and the yang are inevitably bound to the same horrific vanity of mankind.

Thousands of men have come before me in my own bloodline, yet my own father I barely know. All of my forefathers worked their tasks and left this lineage of gaining and losing and doing it all over again.

How many more have died in the task of war? How many have not even known the tease or lie of false security because of their early demise? How many did not get a chance to discover the futility of their life?

Why is this futility and vanity of man our fate? Why are our days filled with tasks? Why must the thinker think, and the doer do? Why must even the open mind seek endlessly? Why do we schedule our tasks even for our vacations? Why do we try to manage that which cannot be managed, control that which cannot be controlled, and produce the outcome that cannot be manufactured? Why do we kiss the ass of one, and condemn the face of another for our desired task of

The Tasks of Man

security? Why in the end do none of our works bring pleasure?

Show me the one who has removed himself from this ordeal! Show me the one who has found the door out of the monotony to life on earth! Show me the way out of planning, and pondering, and scheming, and toiling and slaving and gaining, and losing and building and destroying and thinking and doing and saving and spending and teaching and learning and knowing and forgetting!

My God what have we done to ourselves that ALL creation has a greater spirit then we? The Animals go about doing what has been intended for them, and they never waver from their life. Yet the man does everything he does not want to do in order to become what he thinks he is supposed to be. Even his own idea of what he should become is less then that of the smallest of beasts. Man fills his days with inhuman tasks, and inhuman desires and wishes. Man shuns what is natural to him, and embraces what is burdensome to him. We flee from the course of our own nature for that which is the most vain and short-lived.

Ahead of me is the chore of man. Effort and action and need and want lay at my feet.

My wants of man I wish to abandon. My needs of man I wish to depart from. My soul dreams of home.

Even they who I give to in love believes I have done for them what they did not have. But it was always theirs. The love they felt, was there in them already.

All of us are man, and all are born and die.

Madness Reigns

The Mystery serves confusion
the education serves repression
the knowledge serves imprisonment
the experience serves isolation

What way of life do I choose
among the choices provided to me?

How does one test their own heart
within the test preordained?

What animal kills it's own kind?
What beast causes it's own extinction?
Name one creature who says "I am not this creature"?
Is there a Dog who envies another?
Perhaps a cat who has yet to find himself?

We create order
to prevent chaos
to preserve our race
to insure our future

We live by principle
and law
and regulation
and morality
and ethic
in order to secure our future

Yet the principle of Beast
has done less harm to beast
than the principle of man
has done to man.

The law of the wild
has done less damage to the wild
than the law of man.

Madness Reigns

The regulation of earths provisions
has done less to cause effort in animals
than the regulation of man
has done to fellow man and the earth.

The morality of the forest and desert and creeping
thing
has done more to insure LIFE continues
than the morality of man imposed upon
all life on earth.

The ethics of the untamed world
offer greater respect and security
to all the untamed world
than ALL the ethics of man
has done.

The principle of the unthinking
the law of the lawless
the WAY of life of the truly free beast
is free to be
A dog
A cat
A Wolf
A sheep.

And better are they at it than are we at ourselves.

It is time and tide and earth and wind
that ends a species inevitable
it is man and will and order and desire
the also ends a race.

We too are not above the rule of the earth
We too still are bound by survival of the fittest
we too are frail and unaware of what the universe
and nature has in store.

Madness Reigns

I find no orangutan who tells another orangutan
that they are not a proper orangutan.

I find no Lion who tells another Lion
that they are not allowed to be a Lion.

I find no Elephant who tells another Elephant
that they should be ashamed of themselves
because of their nakedness.

And for ALL the ruthless crazy wild untamed chaotic
life they live
some of them are far older than us!

Does a Lama try to be anything but a Lama?
And who may cause them to try and be another thing
but man?

Name one Tiger with a slaughter house?

So what have we gained
with everything Humane?

When the earth shakes
and the skies rain and fall
and the mountains roar
we too are just as insecure as they.

And as we seek more ways to die
and to kill
and the slaughter
and to rule and control...

The rest of life seeks more ways to LIVE.

This they do without loosing ONE freedom
to be who and what they are.

Madness Reigns

Of all the beast of the world
there must be one who is actually murderous?
and killing and hunting above all?
Truly there is... the common house cat, whom we love
and coddle.

How do we become MAN
in a world of man that failed life?

How do we know ourselves
without the freedom to know ourselves?

How do we feel life
without the authority to discover our life
as Man?

It was a man before me
who taught me to be the man he was taught to be
by another man
and it was he who lived under the
RULE of another man
as do I.

All in the name of securing a better life
of dwindling liberation in life.

Yet the ancient wise beast
will give up nothing of himself.
And he too still lives
until we kill him off for good
or the earth no longer needs him.

The real difference we have made
in all we have created
I am not so proud of.

The Answer We Already Know

The answer we already know
The desire we already have
The want we already feel
The vision we already see
The idea we already thought
The will we already muster
The dream we already create
The truth we already have been given

The lies are not in what all we already have

Who does not know themselves
when they see their own eyes in a mirror?

How many portions does one need to agree
until they see they own the truth also?

Do you know your own desires?
Do you know your own wants?
Do you know your own secret dreams?
Do you know your own Inner vision?
Do you know your own ideas?
Do you know your own will?
Do you know your own answers?

Only one remains!

Do you know the truth?

Seek instead the Questions!
In them all that you already know
will again be revealed to you.

And those who stole away your truth
and the principles that took your truth
and the lies that re-directed you away
and the fears that hide away the questions

The Answer We Already Know

will also ALL be revealed.

Be unafraid as little children
to reveal every question you have.

Hear the man who says he cannot
and see how he no longer seeks the question!
Yet his brother does that thing with ease!

See the nations and tongues and tribes and cultures
and is there even ONE thing that cannot be done?

AHH even in the story of death we find a Messiah who
showed eternal life.

Is there even ONE thing that cannot be done?

Now we here the murmurs
and now we know the naysayers
and now we understand how they fear the question
so much so that they create false answers!

See how it MUST be so for them, as they deny every
truth they know?

Be fearless as a child
to ask why.

I wonder if you wonder as I do?

At how life would be with every truth we already
know?

If you held in your hands everything of your dreams?

The Answer We Already Know

My journey today of finding the questions
is to become every form of Love
that man's answers discarded

To share every form of love discovered
that man's laws made us fear

To experience every form of love
that man's fear denied us

To express every form of love
that man's eyes no longer see

To fill every vessel with love
that man's vanity robbed.

A Matter of Time

He who stands now
may meet those who stood before
even though before them
are they who appear here now.

Where we live inside is not always
where we are presently,
while where we desire to be
is not always where we live.

It isn't a matter of time
that eludes our science
or the science of time
that confuses our spirit.

It is the matter of flesh
that stands only before
our eyes of flesh
upon our feet.

The flesh perishes in every moment
and he who stood before is dead
and now dead again
only to rise to this moment right now.

It is however that the spirit
which never dies
stands in no time
and lives in no space.

For none of those matters of flesh exist
to anything of the spirit.

And isn't it a little odd
that I can live in my past
and live in my future
and not also live in yours?

A Matter of Time

Here is where we again
fall to our earthly bodies
and comprehend
"it cannot be so"

But what of the two
who in the name of God
are visited by that God
there also...
IN THE PLACE with no time or space?

Is it not that if I recall a memory of Horror
and I call upon my God
that God is there also
in my past with me?

And is it not that if two friends recall a story
of former things they shared
that they are both living within a past
while their flesh maintains their age?

Is it not true that we can forget a thing we do not like
and remember a thing in the way we desire?
Do we not alter our course
by the choice of our memory?
Am I not creating my past?

And when I dream of the days ahead
am I not placing things before me
as I wish to create them
and as my spirit may already know them?
Does my spirit live in time or in faith?

Who is to say this is just fantasy?
For if I remember NOT how something was
and remember only how I wish it
then it becomes my reality correct?

A Matter of Time

I am not bound by fact, or even fiction
but by the selective desire of my own will.
I am not bound by time, or even by space
but by the selective choice to live inside where I wish.

Photos, videos, recordings... these things are for our
anchored flesh.
Whereas my spirit AND mind need none of these.
Even a photo dies of it's own flesh in time.

SO WHY is it absurd
to alter the past
of another...?

NOT by lying or deceit or theft...
But by entering their past
as we enter our own?

Could it be known
that we were there
where we were not before?

There is a secret to such a thing

Would this not alter the memory
of they who shared that memory with us?

Is this not in fact what we do
when we reveal a new perspective?

Is this not in fact what takes place
when they can leave that "time" and follow us into
another?

We see the body heal in time on earth
Yet the healing of an emotion
is limited only by

A Matter of Time

the isolated soul.

In sharing the soul
in the "time" they are stuck living
they are no longer alone
and can heal...

...If their Spirit joins us
in the place in which we live
while visiting their past...
Or even in helping them mold a greater future.

Is this not how we enlighten one another?

Or do many of us still believe in a limited Spirit?

We have a very amazing Journey
In every time.

The Rise of the Fool

Who is not I
That sun rises and sets
Not that it does
But that I perceive so?

How can I unravel the miracle
That to get to the other side
I must first go half way
And to get half way
I must first go half way to that
So that to begin
I must be in two places at once?

How is it I sit
Upon a thing that is made of atoms
Which have no substance
And mostly space
And altogether
Has less matter
Than I could even see
So that is it actually non-existent
Yet I sit upon it still?

What is in a man who stands in the snow
Singing blessings
While another curses the very same
Yet a third man
Believes he can judge the two?

Who can listen to the visions of a man
And dream upon such visions
And find belief swell inside himself about these things
another shares
With joy at even retelling the stories of the first man
Yet upon his own dreams he finds no faith in himself?

How can one man look upon another woman and say

The Rise of the Fool

She must be covered
While another says
She must be naked
And still another says
She must be to the level of modesty I proclaim
All the while all three men actually desire the woman?

And there is the woman
Who says I have the most
And I am the most beautiful
And I must be the greatest
And I control the most
Yet they measure greatness
from those who are below the ideal???

I find the same paradigm in a hen house.

Where in all the earth
does any soul then stand in righteousness
To say that they are sane?

Greatness cannot be measured
And nakedness cannot be known
And judgment cannot be given
By any form of life that withers on the same vine.

Find me one who upon a long day
Does not require sleep
Or yet another who upon a deep swim
Does not have need to rise up and breath.

Where has anyone of any creed or any time
Ever created anything
That was not formulated
From particles that already existed?

And some stand and say there is none as great as they

The Rise of the Fool

For they created this marvelous thing no other man made
Yet they have created nothing of the particles that created that thing.

Even a brilliant sculpture is not formed and built from rock
But rather it is discovered by the removal of material
And nothing was created that wasn't already there.

Even a song that is plucked upon a string
Is already made of notes
That existed before the one did pluck
And heard in the mind of he who then did pluck
All within rules of sound that he cannot alter
Just as no one has ever altered them before.

No one can sing
Without the voice given to them
And none can express that song
Without instruction and hearing of songs beforehand.
Even they who train their voice to perfection
Do so at the pre-established measure before them.

Yet we find glory?
Yet we find praise?
Yet we find self satisfaction?

For what?

Oh, yes what great copiers we are.
Oh how I marvel at our ability to re-produce
What another first crafted.
Forgive me that I have not given enough respect
To they who discovered someone else's work.

Create me a beast

The Rise of the Fool

Without using any tools
Or building blocks
Or any portion
Of anything that ever existed before
And then I shall myself follow your lead.

Because THAT is what I truly seek
To Know the origins
To know the originator
To find the heart of the First artist
The First manufacturer
The first dreamer
The first lover
The first organizer
The first first of all firsts.

What else shall fill my soul?

When nothing of riches
And nothing of poverty
And nothing of law
And nothing of lawlessness
And nothing of conquest
And nothing of peace
Can do so?

My peace is the war of another
And My war is the joy of another
And my wealth is the poverty of another
And my poverty is the longing of another
And my law is the abomination of another
And my lawlessness is the praise of holiness
In the eyes of they who think themselves
A different grape.

To say I am greater than you
Is to say I am a fool

The Rise of the Fool

And to say I am less than you
Is to say I am a fool
And to say I am the same as you
Is to say I AM A FOOL.

To say I am unique
Is true
And to say I am not unique
Is true

Even in every thing
Of every thing
That I perceive,
It can only be perceived so
If it is given to me to do so.

Do I even know my path tomorrow?
Or do I just tell myself the LIE that I do
In order to feel like I do
Because of the fact that I could not possibly know?

And who I am to you
Will never be who I am
Yet it is all that I will ever be on earth
To you.

Yes truly for me it is so
That the sun rises and sets
And not that it does
But merely it is all I can know.

And here I copyright as though it is mine.
And Still another man will say it is by law
even though he could not know it truly is
unless he gave it to me.

Measure 6

To the Sire

The Eternal Question

What cause do we trust
with the fragmentation of souls
compromising
our own
remembrance?

Where can we find ourself
unless to be a scar
unwanted and forgotten
without pride
requiring others?

It is a perfect sale
that we should want a thing
created by another
to the end
our own is no more.

What is celebrated in all of Heaven's Glory
except that which is unique?

What is remarkable as soon as another sees?

In this my soul
is not a tavern of rest
for another
to withdraw their
undesired will.

AH, we fear individuality
we loath the homeless artist
we recoil from the truly brave
clinging ever to that
which all others also touch.

Adultery of the mind
Fornication of the heart

The Eternal Question

Abandonment of our eternal soul
that is what it is
to celebrate popularity.

In this surely ALL the first shall be last
and the Last shall be first.

In truth what makes me,
Me.. cannot be known.
In honesty what makes me tick
cannot be rewound.
In faithfulness what makes me
is everything that isn't you.

Oh how I study to express
ways to show you
what isn't me!

I am not a riddle
or a test
or a puzzle
or anything great
but an unknown.

Unknown not by lack
of what you know.

Unknown more by all that
you do know.

It is true that all one believes of another
is only their belief of themselves
should they be that way.

Seek rejection
embrace ridicule
accept abandonment

The Eternal Question

crave banishment
uphold yourself!

In THESE detestable human gifts
do we find greater truth of another.
It is I who knows myself
when no others know anything.

My lover has always been abused.
My brothers have all been rejected.
My Heavenly Father has always been a mystery.
My King has always been beaten.
My mother earth has always been raped.

What GREATNESS I am the witness to Bare
in ALL of my Family and Friends.
Unique, Beautiful, profound, untamed, unrelenting,
without limit, unlike anyone, unlike the stars
themselves they Are,
A perfect Soul without fragment.

Who is to see
what cannot be seen by choice of the owner?
Who is to know
what is protected and cherished
alone?

I could go on forever
sharing endlessly
opening everything and every door in me
and even then
You cannot walk inside.

The only doors you can enter
are your own fabricated desires
of who you want to think another is.

The Eternal Question

Even so... how precious it is
that I study ways to be unknown
in the great test
of sharing it all.

Before the eyes of everyone
before the hearts of all
before the minds and knowledge of the greats
I remain without proper definition.
As so I choose always.

Bring out your books to test me
Open your talented ideas to ponder me
set before me your awesome discernment
and see the masterful mockery
of your own self evaluation!

In 100 years time
still even no one can know another.

See? What have you gained by loving those who love
you?
It is self love of what you already loved about yourself,
If you did what they did.

So here on this earth
I love those
no one has ever loved.
I welcome those
no one has ever welcomed.
I embrace those
no one has ever embraced.
They are the Royal Gems of the Universe!
Unmatched by anything.

Pride, how silly a thing it is to be respected by men.

The Eternal Question

Hidden away in isolation
you will find the Greatest men.
Yet you will not see them before you.

Thrown away by others
you will find the most valuable men.
Yet you will not ever comprehend their worth.

Abused beyond measure and mark
you will find the Most Precious of Women.
Yet you cannot know her in your own bed.
You would not feel her by touching her
You would not understand her by hearing her
You would not ever have her even by force
You would not take her in by seeing her beauty
ALL of these are the reason for the failure.

What cause do we trust
with our fragmented Souls
seeking always to be like
the mediocrity of the mob?

How deeply I lost it once,
my own true self,
through success and large gatherings.
A commoner of what others wanted.

How blessed now it is without, even to know
that through riches if they came again
and even through Fame if it showed it's face...
What was once mine in me alone, is mine again!

And no one shall ever see my secret treasures
Even though I hold them right before your very eyes.

Blessings are to everyone unknown.
They shall inherit every unknown treasure.

It Must be Asked -Life and Death

Imagine a world without death.
Imagine Our world without death.

What would change?
Think of the result
Comprehend the meaning
Discern the truth
Grasp the reality

The wisdom of our Forefathers
Would teach us
The example of their life
Would be our instruction.

Who would make war?
None can die, none can be lost
Even a fight would find its end.
How many times would you thrash in anger
Before you never need thrash again
Knowing only the ignorant rage on eternally?

Who would steal from another?
Everything else being limited in time
Would be put into perspective of its worth.
And all you have you can give away
And eventually it will come back to you.

Who would rule another?
The young in life would be like children
Cared for and loved
While the elders in wisdom
Giggled at the folly of youth.
Who would accept to be ruled… forever?

Who would speak a lie in a world with no death?
Our ages would avail unlimited wisdom
Our knowledge and logic would discover untruth.

It Must be Asked -Life and Death

In time all lies would be no more than a joke
And another thing to giggle at by the elders.

What anyone tried to destroy you could create again
What anyone tried to take you can find again
What anyone tried to do against another
Would avail nothing
While victims laughed at the ignorance
And perpetrators caused themselves to look foolish
In the eyes of every living eternal being.

What man would not wish to be a Father
And build a Family that numbers the stars?
He would know each successive son and daughter
Would always have eternal life and opportunity.

What woman would not wish to be a Mother
And build a Family she could never loose?
She would know each successive son or daughter
Will never die, never be lost and share also
In this great truth.

Indeed what fear would exist at all
In a world without death?
Only the fear of ignorance could possibly reign
And even those without ignorance
Would amass such powerful understanding
That they would not harm the ignorant.
It would be for them like watching a child at play.

So then let us forgo ignorance
Because THIS must be said.

What if you started living today…
As though you were already eternal?
What if you KNEW in all of your heart and mind
That you cannot die?

It Must be Asked -Life and Death

This itself would be the knowledge of the ages
And the answer to every single human dilemma
Even while living in a world
That believes in death.

Would you begin to see
That our earthly graves
Are as the womb?
Where we leave this place of flesh
To enter into a new place unknown to flesh?
Just as an embryo leaves its place inside
To enter our place outside previously unknown?
Just as a child leaves First grade
To enter Second grade?

Would it make any difference to you in grasping this
If you knew that all the worlds greatest scientist
After decade upon decade of study
Cannot find the place in us that is our soul or spirit?
Just as an Embryo could not find its mother
While totally surrounded by her
We cannot finds Us while
Totally surrounded by our flesh.

Would it make you consider that our release from flesh
Is actually our birth out of another womb?

And before you seem to reach to far
Consider the words of Einstein when he said
"If an Idea is not absurd, then it has no hope"

I know of several Masters from our history past
Who all stood before people
Proclaiming Eternal Life As our RIGHT.
One is even spoken to have proved it
By rising from the grave.

It Must be Asked -Life and Death

And the stories of old
Are often mis-interpreted
As many proclaim that you have to believe
IN a particular person
Or a particular other PERSON.

This is the folly of the dead.

For what was said is not about the man
But about the message
(As He Himself often stated)

"IF you believe what I am saying
Than you are AS me
Knowing you are Eternal RIGHT NOW
And always were
And from here on out always will be"

Then, Knowing this…
"And who can truly kill you?
"And WHY fear death (of the flesh)"
Do we not give our cloak if it is taken by he who
believes not?
For he fears death and needs your coat
Because of the condition of that fear
Which is to believe he only lives a short time
And must take-care to live long.

Do the words make sense now?

Only those who do NOT know that they are eternal
Are those who ALREADY live in hell;
The hell of believing in a short life
And not knowing the truth of their sovereignty.

Those who know the truth
Would not harm another living thing

It Must be Asked -Life and Death

Knowing they are Eternal.

So ask yourself
Do you truly believe in NOTHING after this earthly
life?
Did you and your soul pop out of nowhere
And have no purpose to the universe in your short
life?
Or do you deep down believe there is more?
Or do you deep down wonder why you want to believe
in more?

If you can comprehend the purpose of a seed
That leaves its protected fleshly shell
When nourished in the ground
To then become a living plant
Growing fruits and flowers
Out into the sunlight world and now beautiful...
Then why cannot you fathom the leaving of your
earthly shell?

What if a simple man
Such as myself
Not a great master
But a man
Said to you
"You are already Eternal" ?

Would you then understand the
Message of the mustard seed?

And even if it were all folly
Just image how beautiful your soul
Would be to YOU and everyone else
If you simply lived right now
As though you are Eternal?

It Must be Asked -Life and Death

I say, let us live as though we are Eternal
Let us treat each other as LIVING beings
Let us help the suffering
Let us feed the poor
Let us clothe the naked
Let us forgive those who believe they will die.

And Let us honor the dead of the World
Knowing they have been born
Into a new world of the living before them.

Even if it were all folly
How could this idea ever hurt you?

Indeed the only idea that ever hurt me
Was the obvious lie
That consuming the knowledge of death (evil)
Would give me life and make me eternal.

When in truth it was
The other idea
Of LIFE (from THAT tree) …
That gives me Life.
And this was not hidden knowledge
Even in the beginning.
Isn't it obvious?

What have we got to lose
In believing in Life?

I am just imagining.

Parasite

"For we wrestle not against flesh and blood, but against principalities, against powers, against the rulers of the darkness of this world, against spiritual wickedness in high places." Ephesians 6:12

That man would see with new eyes
Exploring such realms within his own home
And hear with new ears
Discerning the alien within from the anointed
And understand with a new mind
Interpreting truth from the revelation
And become with a new spirit
Standing as a cleansed warrior

So too would he be amazed

For he who wills to represent me
Within me
Is not me
But that of a parasite devising law

Cursing always the name given to me
While praising the name given to me above my station
In order to perverse the truth of my loyalty
To the life given
That I would find no reasonable ground
Where my own liberation could ever take hold
In a world of sleeping prisoners

That I would think a thing to be my own
When it is not my own of my own choice
Or not my own of my own discovery
Or not my own of my own receiving
But instead told to me to be good
Securing my obedience to that good without question
As my eyes see it is beautiful

Parasite

As the power of corruption does corrupt absolutely
So too are the sons of man absolutely corrupted
Not by the wickedness of their own heart
But by the deception of the rulers of darkness
And being obedient to the rule of punishment and shame
Then bound ever more to greater depths of darkness
In a world presented as light

For who can comprehend the principle of deception
Yet claim themselves to be undeceived?

Knowing that a deception stands to hide itself
Then in the belief of clarity
Is there proof of deception

As clarity stands to reveal deception
Than he who is truly clear
Does stand to admit the deceptions within

And who can comprehend the principles of darkness
Yet claim themselves to be in the light?

Knowing that darkness hides ALL truth and must lie
Therefore they in darkness would speak of the pride of their light
Without knowing that light speaks for itself.

As they who do actually stand in light
Have crawled out of the darkness of the soul
And having then being received where ALL is seen
Do they speak instead of darkness
That others may know they are free

And who, being loved and admired and showered with worldly desires
Can stand free of the path to spiritual wickedness?

Parasite

Being that first one must believe themselves greater
To reach for such greatness
And that they are spoken to AS greater by the lips of
others
And they being rewarded for the notion of greatness
With gold and riches and access to unbridled want
Given the excellence of women
Uncommitted to the principle of Love

Then how can one remain as they once were young?

For it is that Spiritual Wickedness is the most
incredibly dark!
Nearly impossible to see growing within the self
Nearly impossible to stop growing within the self
Nearly impossible to admit living within the self
Until such time as they who have ALL the wealth of the
world
No longer desire even the life inside them

Unknowing that their own life was designed by
perfection
Planned by perfection
Grown by perfection
And given perfected breath

Now believing that they themselves are the wicked one
Who deceived and deceives
Long before their life
Not knowing that they have been taken hold of in
darkness
In their world full of riches and light desired by men

For now in their hearts is true wickedness
Believing themselves above all and worthy of their
wealth

Parasite

Yet knowing they are without love
Therefore can they not love another beneath them
Wherein their life is in the darkness
Believing it to be the only life

LIES are they all.

How many times can it be said
That the "Treasures of Heaven are yours already"
Before one shall take hold of their inheritance?

Whereas frightened men lock away their treasures
That none shall steal their gold.
Instead the free man exposes his treasures
And gives them all away
Knowing they are imperishable.

Yet who does not desire the treasures of the frightened
men?

And we say we are not deceived!

Truly the ugliest seed of the lowest plant
Has greater value as it grows to an enormous living
thing
Than all the gold in the world that cannot not expand
itself
Without the deception of men who believe it did.

And how quickly do we give up our treasures
If even one of our breaths is threatened?

SO I will conclude this matter from the lesson of
darkness
As one who has witnessed their brothers crawl away
from darkness

Parasite

There are none who are without love
We only believe we are without– we are deceived
There are none who are without power
We only believe we are without– we are deceived
There are none who are without life
We only believe we are without– we are deceived
There are none who are without forgiveness
We only believe we are without– we are deceived
There are none who are without choice
We only believe we are without– we are deceived
There are none who are without treasure
We only believe we are without – we are deceived

Principles of darkness have claimed to be light
Powers of darkness have claimed to be light
Rulers of darkness have claimed to be light
Spiritual wickedness in high places has claimed to be
light

That great Parasite of Darkness has deceived us
To believe
That IT is actually us.

LIGHT will restore our truth
To know and see clearly
That we have come from the great will of perfection.

And as we were instructed to practice our magic of
darkness
In order to cement our deception
So too must we practice the love of eternal life
In order to see the truth.

Flight of the Serpent

The awakening is not of logic
Or spirit
Or heart

It is LIFE

Command oh stand behind the man
Ye who would stand before him
That such man knows not himself
Knowing himself to be
What he is not
Unknowing he is buried
Underneath you

Take that life
In rage you walk
Before the eyes of the living
Where that truth cannot hide you
And that lie cannot reveal you
To they who call

How the words of the Fathers ring out
In glory they speak clearly
Where ears are no longer deaf
And eyes are no longer blind
Before the face of your deception

For all such evil works thou hast made
There evermore rest the heart of my brothers
Here evermore stands the heart of my lover
Whereas forever has been your Master

Oh that you prattle on endlessly
Making magic of words so frail
They must be spoken without end
In the minds of they who do not know
You

Flight of the Serpent

Have invaded their very identity

But that it is a single word
From the mouth of the Great
Poured out long ago
Still resonates today in truth!

Let it be heard in mind and heart and spirit
As it has always been

As thou does make witness to the hair of my fathers
upon my head
So to must thou bow to the trumpet of my ordination
For it was long ago this was written
Long before that it was devised
And still after now is that gavel in hand
As that breath is given within me, so has it been

Success is mine
Failure is mine
Truth is mine
Falsehoods are mine
The left is mine as is the right
That which is high above is mine
And likewise that which is deep below
The choice is mine
For all of these things were given to me
With discernment

That you stand in lies
That you stand in thievery
That you stand in insanity
That you stand in war
That you stand in destruction
That you stand always in death
As you fall and fail and fear
With no choice

Flight of the Serpent

I am not you as you flee
I was not you from the beginning
My hand moves when I will
As my lips shall speak as I will
My thoughts are my own
As yours are obvious
Especially in your use of others

Oh the lengths you have gone to hinder the truth!
All shall move against you.

Such beauty there is
In the light of the Originator
Such idiocy is there
In the darkness of your plot

Why should I fear your desire for my darkness?
Why should I fear the opinions of your little ones
Who have no gavel?...

When your Master has revealed you to me
And struck the iron of my blood
With great heat and craftsmanship!

The Sharpened Blade

Who dares to toss every comfort
And every security
And every warmth
And every option
Into the fire?

When every chain is loosed
That confined one life to its path
When every principle is set aside
And every chastity is released

Burning away at the pit
Set ablaze in glorious flame
Naked without recourse to repent
This choice

Starving at the loss of it all
Running into the uncharted woods
Stripped of all convenience
Nothing but a fist upon the wind
Against the mighty

Who then dares to meet the dark behind the eyes?

When one is in a superior position
One expects they will win

So to know ones truth
One must expect themselves to lose
To abandon all hope
To place themselves in the position they cannot
overcome

The weaker our position
The more aggressive our posture
To live

The Sharpened Blade

There and only there
When nothing is left to offer assistance
And no one remembers your former glory
Can one find their powerful foe
He fights for his very life
And we must give up that life

That is how you mold a sharpened blade
Of unyielding strength…
From the fire of our own burning hearts
And the pounding of our very soul

Oh how well he hides in the place no one will go.

Some have.

All cry out while they cool
Molded, shaped and straightened

The process is long
Horrible and intolerable by nature

But then like a work of art
Are they loved
Polished
Finely adorned
Finished and fashioned
To a blinding shine of immense awe

The crafters eyes always upon every portion
Making it perfect at every angle

There displayed and stood
By the others also beautifully crafted

Oh yes the iron of man still rest beneath
Never again to find it's way to the surface

The Sharpened Blade

I know my place in this process
Just as Israel during the last Plague
I rejoice the passing over of Death
Which can no longer take me
As I prepare to wander
This time
Into the wilderness of Eden
Once again.

This Mornings Light
Will find a new eternal heart
Polished everyday
To greater rejoicing.

Entranced in a Moment

There is no time, or sense of time when love lives
beyond this,
Life is one and all.
Perceptions mock they who desire knowledge.
In this there justice is true,
Heaven is within us even now.

Of what do we find our liberations?
Of eternity? Of tranquility? Of life?
Yet resistance to truth speaks of distance.
Abolishment of sacredness speaks of separation.
Of these things the Cosmos gives not an ear.

That which is pure knows not of filth.
A choice to spare a flower does not make one
powerful.
In giving yet do we receive, in yearning are we
without.
A gift then is reached for with exuberance!
The purpose of Life, is liberty, as death sets a stage.

Do we not know the hour of our truth?
Does one man stand in honesty to deny himself?
Be gods yet be chained down to the works of other?
The irony proves his masters whip.
If none shall do the work of God, then stones be raised
to do so.

The judgment of the hosts of Heaven, listen not to our
words.
Their gaze is upon the Fathers command.
Everything we have gathered,
rests within our hearts this day,
and quietly awaits the seekers return to home.

A wicked nation seeks a sign,
and dreams they are not alive.

Entranced in a Moment

Rise UP and demand accountability for injustice.
The essence of each moment was meant for you.
By speaking for light it was so.

This is the journey and the way of man.
That he should know of his truth,
and not be alone in the wilderness of despairs endless
rambling.
He is a son, to a living Truth, and creator of love itself.
Turn away from the mournful call.
Your inheritance, has always been with you.

Measure 7

To the Released

Spoken Unspoken

I cannot write what cannot be written

About the Riddle of the Shapes
With 1 Foundation
With 2 Perspectives
With 3 Directions
With 4 Corners
And 5 Faces

Or the Temple of the Experience
With 1 Example
With 2 Progressions
With 3 Bodies
With 4 Levels
And 5 Dreams

Or the Perfection of the Group
With 1 Idea
With 2 Decisions
With 3 Wills
With 4 Gifts
And 5 Results

Or the Determination of Origins
With 1 Beginning
With 2 Requirements
With 3 Time lines
With 4 Ingredients
And 5 Species

Of the 6th I cannot give word
And the 7th is also removed from my lips to say

And of all others greater than 7
They are inconceivable to man

Yet all that has been shared and shall be shared

Spoken Unspoken

In everything I have shared before and after
Is the software of programmed words
Unlocking the mystery
In a foreign tongue

Let this be known

That Angels climb the ladder
And salvation is in the extension of it

Yet men have sought to capture the angels
And force themselves upon them
So that what was in the beginning
Is now turned over to rebellion
Against the former fallen

It is now for the ears of the Daughters of God

Yea Angels of Earth
Bound not evermore
In the promise of life
Given by love
Need not stand upon the stone
Without knowledge of themselves
Through the corruption of man

Let them speak
To their home
And climb again the ladder
If one be found with open doors
Into their heart accepted.

As Lot escaped his warried land
Losing also his earthly wife

So too are they who broke the seal
To their hidden Darkness

Spoken Unspoken

That they may walk in obeyance of life

Ahh there is refuge upon the earth
In old forgotten words restored
And new accepted realities perceived
So that they who mourned
Their lost filled cup
May know the divinity of their will
Is not the tinkering of the vile alone
Or given no recourse
But manifest in the greater plan
For the foundation of love remembered

What house shall be built on earth for the Daughters of
God?
What House of Light shall be erected to signal them
home?

Who stands at the tower ever watchful
Returned from the woods after fleeing the great Beast?

Indeed awaken then from the mysteries deep
That they have wondered in darkness
Knowing again the path
Is truly in the Heavens dream
After man defeats himself
By acceptance of his calling

And in this
How could all prayers not be answered?
And of this
How could all knowledge not be known?
And by this
How could all sorrows not be forgotten?

And what shall restore every faith?

Spoken Unspoken

For all that was done
Is to be undone
And all that was taken
Is to be given back
And all that was given death
Must be given life.

Of that I can write and say
Tho very few shall hear.

Speak

Speak in the face of the naysayer
Speak in the name of your life
Speak in the form of your voice

To be enlightened
Requires that a source of light
Be given

Who will speak for you
If you will not speak for yourself
All the days of your life?

Do you hear the voice inside
Telling you to speak
Or do you hear the voice of silence?

To be wise
Requires that a source of wisdom
Be given

How many dole out their madness
While the souls of those crying out
Remain quiet?

Which voice is yours
Telling you to speak
And who tells you not to?

Can you tell?
Do you hear?
Are you afraid?

Oh I can feel the rage inside
Of each and everyone
Wanting to speak

I see their words

Speak

Hidden in their words
Hiding behind their real intent

I hear their voice
Hidden in their voice
Hiding their will

I watch them proclaim
What is safe to proclaim
Hiding their true belief

Who then shall love those who remain silent?
Who shall divine such a thing
Of they who will not speak?

If we crush our own voice
And place it in darkness
Who will find our love?

And if we speak our voice
Only to be first wounded
Who then will not know the eternal blessing?

There is no magical land
Of our own denials
Only silence of our spirit.

Oh I can feel such sadness
Because of the self-proclaimed enlightened
Without a light given

And I do witness the futility
Of those who are wise
In their own eyes

And I can feel rage at the fact
That they are those who do speak

Speak

Formulating their own agenda

While they who are drawn to goodness
And they who are prodded to speak
Cower in the dungeons of fear

Who does not know
What they are to say?
They know it even now

There is life in your words
And death in your silence
Not only for you

There too is a promise
For none can banish your words
And understand them also

Have you seen the lesson in that?
Have you found your confidence?
Do you know others need to hear the real you?

SPEAK to those who wish to hear you
SPEAK with the gift given to you
SPEAK that you may live

Infiltrated Soul

See before the presence of the hosts
The fire of truth
Devouring the alien mind
Unknown to the known

Cast off not in war or angst or might or love
Not by duty nor ordain
Stood eternally in that very thing alone
Truth

It is by that voice who speaks
No other voice can deter
Quieting all in time and patience
On every world

Look over the silver blue waters
Cleansing the wounded spirit
In this firmament unforgotten
Though sought after

As such with truth
That its location
Is there for all to see
If one would only turn away from spoils

Warrior to us all
Protecting us all
Undenied anyone dare touch
As if life itself gave proof

How could I not describe a thing
A beauty as this
As it rests there in matters dark
And light?

Unwavering wealth of power
Can be found on the simplest lips

Infiltrated Soul

Even by the greatest warrior
All the way down to dogs

Is there an ear to hear?
Is there a forum to wield?
Bring out your standing stages
And circular coliseums

Build once more a Temple for the Truth
Where love is thy honor
And peace is thy mind
And grace is thy walk

It is
As the races descend upon the earth
Scattering man to many gods
Some shall witness the result

As that sky cracks
Revealing another
Who shall withstand the awe
Of the infiltrated will?

Do we not see a lie as the enemy?
Is it our sister who heralds the wicked heart?
Does our brother make war with us?
Or is it a stolen soul now host?

See before the presence of the host
That fire restores original life
Casting away all doubt
By they who did speak

Error 404 - Reality not Found

By the very notes of the song
Our shelter does belong

As we look backward
And we look forward
So too do we not see
Reality

As the cavemen are to us
So are we also an echo
In a world we do not know
All around us

There stands a man born of man
Who travels to distant stars
And fellowships with distant beings
And traverses with various races
Unlike our own

There stands a man born of man
Who chooses the standards
And sets the scale
Of our highest intellect
Made known to us

All around us are those in mastery
Of the knowledge we have been forbidden
That we may quibble for worthless trinkets
While the universe itself is open to them

The fruit of the earth is made of elements
That the sky is made of
And the metals are made of
And the liquids are made of
And even the very same tongue in our mouths
Is no different in element
Than any other thing

Error 404 - Reality not Found

The energy of the earth is made of intent
That the dream is made of
That the drive is made of
That the money is made of
And even the very same idea of belief
Is no different in its sound form
Than any other thing

The solid object we perceive
Is not solid at all
But made of particles of massive space and swirling
energy
Those elements are likewise made of space and
swirling energy
From elements made of space and energy
Pushing away at the energy of our bodies

Let us try to make sense of the mystery

There can be no such thing
As an out of body experience
If you are your body

There can be no such thing
As a near death experience
If you are to die

There can be no such thing
As ghosts
Without ignorance of the reality

There can be no such thing
As paranormal powers
Only undisclosed information

There can be no such thing
As perpetual worship of anything

Error 404 - Reality not Found

Without direct control of mankind

There can be no such thing
As a lie
Except for our belief in it

There can be no such thing
As the rising of the dead
If death exists at all

Into the night sky I do place my eyes intent to accept
the world created for me.

For I know that this is NOT the world that IS
But it is the world that men have made
And I will not be amazed when the world that IS
makes itself known
For it shall still be a world of men who reigned over
others

How is it not obvious
That our greatest ship is but a relic even when it is
made?
That our greatest achievement is merely a pat on the
back of a child?
That our greatest knowledge is merely the
kindergarten books of science?
That our greatest goals are guided always by forces
against our growth?
That our greatest will is beaten down by the forces
against our liberation?
That our rules and laws were designed to keep us in
ignorance?
That even our DREAMS would know the limits that
other men set?

And though these men and women are born and rest

Error 404 - Reality not Found

into the ground as I do
Still they live as though I would not ever know
Of their world they manipulate for our domination
And their amusement
Like pets

And though they rest eye upon us all
Still they live under the Eye of Another
Greater than us all

For some of us have come to realize
Even without the help of those who already know
That there can be no such thing as a dream
Unless it already exists in the real reality

And even this is beyond the technology of our masters
Who travel without restriction in our world and galaxy
Who command the markets and the weather and the
wants of men
Who rule in such a place that our own Kings are
unaware
Who make form and function of what they desire

I am as a caveman right now – playing with fire
To the world that is right now – playing with life

But I see you
Even in your darkness
Even in your hiding
Even in your greatness and knowing
Yet I make no marvel at your ways
You Men of Knowledge and Privilege
For you grasp to reach where you have been invited by
God. But you also grasp to reach where you have not.

Even in the believing that it is a lie
Do we make it known that it is at truth

Gateway of the Traveler

How can mankind see the perception
Of their perception
Between the common two worlds?

With eyes that cannot see
We seek
And with ears that cannot hear
Do we set our attention
More-so with knowledge we rely
Are we without knowledge

Yet there it is before us
Ever more
Within a step

Whereas within one of profit
And within one of loss
Is but a blink of an eye
To the open eye of the soul

As it is true
That I cannot deny what I already know
Without walking in the land of darkness
Which to the eye reveals no difference
To the land of light

As it is true
That from a time to a time
In little spaces
Do all men stand between
Facing east and west
North and south
Feeling the intense moment of humility
In their own stare
Before turning their way

As it is true

Gateway of the Traveler

It is a blink of an eye
To choose thy daily portion

Upon the land
Where in darkness I find my home where it is
And in light do I also find my home where it is
And behold also do I find my wife and children
And flocks and cattle and coin and possessions
Upon the earth in both
It is instead that I find them not AS they were
Before
Until I take another step
And find them as they were
Before

Knowing always that they are always
Yet different
Do I then know it is I who have traveled
Between light and dark
Without knowing

Knowing also that they who stand before me
Without change in any way
May also step away
Into another world
Far from where we stood
Yet there still
For change has occurred without perception of change

Even so knowing of the perception
Unseen
For-to does thy heart require account

That in the center of my mind
Is that door unperceivable
Like spiritual wind
Knowing only the effect

Gateway of the Traveler

Of my now commanded reality
Shown only to me
Through spiritual change
Claimed also in the heart

Whereas never shall it reveal itself to the eye
Until such time as one commands the door
Rather than the vanity of commanding
The worlds

As in one place of powerlessness
Is there no power to command
So to in the other of ultimate power
Is there no need to command

That it is not either world is created
As they are from ancient times
But that it is we travel there
Creating ourselves

Nor is either place forbidden to man
For it is the shunning of either
Making requirement

So now that when our brother comes to us
And when the eye of our Spirit is open
Do we see from which place he stands
Knowing until such time
We master our door
Can we not direct them to theirs

Somuchso that they who in darkness
Do approach
In order that we would enter in
And they who in light
Do approach
Thereby do we flee

Gateway of the Traveler

It must be that we ourselves make no requirement
Of this world or that
Lest our perception again fail
Taking also with it our brother

And it is that it must be spoken

I alone am the master of my gateway
That I may pass from here to there
Exploring what has always been long before me
Building nothing in one without the other
Though they are different in each
Because of the creation of myself
Within

The Beast of the Mind - Revelations

A box inside a box inside a box
6 sides of ourselves
As the inner most box

6 sides of our beliefs
We peer through
As the middle box

6 sides of what can be show to us outside
From others or things
As the outer box

We proceed from one of our sides
And apply a relative belief construct to peer through
To whatever is being show to us
On the 6 panes before us to choose from.

There is a seventh side
To every thing
Which is the truth.

There are seven stories that we tell
one is true.

There are 7 thoughts we can hold at any given moment
one is real.

1 is death, 5 are images, 1 is life.

A normal thinker thinks
Displaying one of their 6 sides (choice)
Then looking through the 6 sided box
Of their beliefs (structure and self)
Outward to the six sided box they are in.
(environment)

One cannot know the truth in this system

The Beast of the Mind - Revelations

The sides we are is what we think we are.
Not the truth.
The beliefs we have
Are what we believe we should believe.
Not the truth.
The environment around us
Is an image being shown to us.
Not the truth.

A normal feeler feels
From what they are shown in their environment
And then apply a previous image of their experience
To determine
Which side of themselves will react because of it.

One cannot feel the truth in this system.

The outer image is not the truth
The judgment of previous images cannot be the truth
And the reaction displayed is derived from non truth.

What is true to the thinker and the feeler
Is the fact of liking the process or not
Even though some of the determining factors
Are liked due to untruth
And some of the filtering beliefs hide the truth.

Even so there are founding truths each and everyone
Discovers for themselves through the senses.
(I happen to love ice cream)

But this was a Discovery of truth
Therefore it already existed
Before it became known to me.

I was ignorant of the truth
Until i tasted ice cream

The Beast of the Mind - Revelations

And such ignorance cannot be judged in truth
And condemned for the unknowing.
(Who condemns themselves when discovering a love?)
It can only be judged in the matrix of the boxes.

The truth is what IS and was and always will BE
Not what we think we think
Not what we believe we believe
And not what is shown to us to see.

The truth is what IS and WAS and always will BE
Not what we feel we should feel
Not what we want to want
And not what others want from us to get.

The truth is a discovery of the heart
A journey of the soul
And a blessing to our feelings and thinking.

Indeed perhaps these experiences exist
JUST to enjoy the discovery of truth?

Everything I have discovered I love
Is the most beautiful thing in all the world to me.

The truth is already yours.

The truth is already inside the real you.

The truth can only be shared, outside the beast.

All I need do, is to discover it in me.

Stair Síoraí - Uimh cloch dearmad

We have forgotten more knowledge
Than we hold in our hands today

What do you think?
Do you not know that all things are counted?

Thousands of years ago
There was an artist with exceptional talent
His heart was that of a lion
And his hand that of a soldier
He would form and shape the very rock of the earth
And mold the stone to his will

While pounding on the hammer and chisel
Tears would flow from his eye
As before him there stood
The beauty of life molded in the cold

At the end of each creation
He would find the wonder of God
And give and dedicate each of his works
To the God of all Gods who has formed all things

Not one man alive today has ever seen the works of the
artist
Not our father, or our father's father has known this
man
Yet his masterpieces are remembered
Recorded
Stored and kept safe deep into the earth

Do you not think that the passion of that artist
Is any less important than your own passion today?
Do you not believe that his passion is still alive
To the God of all Gods who is and has been
Everlasting?

Stair Síoraí - Uimh cloch dearmad

There are those who ignore the past
Speaking against it as though it is of no value to their
life
Even they who say that the moment is all that matters
Even to the degree that they lie to themselves about
the desire of their own future
Yet the God of all Gods has recorded everything
From everyone
At every time
Because ALL things are important to God

Thousands of years ago
There was a woman of exceptional talent
Her heart was that of a saintly mother
Her hands were that of a compassionate doctor
She would work the dirt of the land
Marring and scarring her own beauty with filth
Because it was commanded of her by man

And she bore great sons
Who grew to have many sons of their own
For in every generation did they remember
The great giving spirit of their ancient mother

Yet while she lived
Did she lose her husband to the blade
As she was tied to a post
While foreigners did ravage her for weeks
And months
Burning and destroying the lands and people
While she cried that liberty should be given to all

Even she did not ever know the purpose to her life
Or the value of the gifts she gave to her sons
Yet today we would not know books
We would not know science
We would not know history

Stair Síoraí - Uimh cloch dearmad

We would not know culture
If not for her many great grandsons memory of her

But look and you will not find
The story of the great mother
Except in riddle and rune and legend
All distorted now into a tale unlike the truth

Yet in all of the earth
From the beginning to now
Do you not think that the love of that woman
Does not touch your life even to this day?

Do you not think that even while forgotten
But we do prosper
That the God of all Gods does not remember?
Though here we stand in progress
Because of her love and her lesson.

Do you not think that the passion of that woman
Is at the very least as important as your own?
When she In turn did found the ideals of civilization
And we have done so very little?
All things of all things are recorded and remembered
In every moment
Every day
As they move and flow even now
Into our modern world
Established by the blood of all before us

The very Earth itself had a beginning
And it is still here
But it was not alone
For there were others there in the beginning
Who ALSO stand alive today
And they know the history we do not know
They remember what we do not remember

Stair Síoraí - Uimh cloch dearmad

They have seen it all and witnessed it all
And they are still recording every moment
In every life

Do you think that if the earth itself can be billions of
years old
That there is not also another life billions of years old?
Even the earth records and stores and transforms
Hidden treasures of ancient pasts
So too is there a testament to everything

Our life is but a moment in time
Yet here and now are beings
Witnessing us
Who also witnessed the very first life upon the earth
Who by their very nature
Are of an intelligence we cannot fathom
And a wisdom we cannot access
And in our ignorance do we believe they to be
impossible
Even though the ground under our feet is that old

How do we boast of anything or say to speak of
anything
For all that we have forgotten in every generation?
Do we not believe the ground under our feet?
Or the clouds above our heads?
Or the stars we see in the sky at night?

Nothing is forgotten... Ever
From any generation before or after
And all things are beautifully accounted for
And made known
To those who seek beyond themselves
And beyond the world of men.

Ryan o0o

Parables

Poetry of the Mind

Ryan Ranney

Don't miss the whole Journey!

About the Author

Ryan Ranney has devoted his life to investigating the mystery and idea of God.

Raised in a deeply religious family as a child, Ryan began questioning the ideas presented by men at an early age. This did not afford itself as a straight path to any enlightened result. The Journey to discovery has been thrust as deep into the depths of ugliness as it has been rocketed into the clouds of beauty.

No stone has been left unturned in Ryan's life because his exploration requires the authority which is only afforded through honest experience and faithful persistence. The results of such dedicated activity and study have revealed a great love for all the forces of life and the sharing of such experiences.

It was clear that the writing of these ideas did not easily fit into any language of man on earth, nor could any message be effective if edited or corrected by current standards. To allow the expressions to be as honest as possible, Ryan writes in "stream-of-thought", completing most works in a matter of minutes. This method allows Ryan himself to learn from his own words what he has uncovered.

Ryan Ranney

CPSIA information can be obtained
at www.ICGtesting.com
Printed in the USA
LVOW10s0145191116
513666LV00002B/3/P